THE ACHIEVEMENT BLUEPRINT

THE ACHIEVEMENT BLUEPRINT

Tactical Strategies for Goal Attainment

INNER POWER

Inner Strength Counselling

CONTENTS

CHAPTER 1

The Power of Purpose

In a notable study conducted in 1979, Harvard MBA graduates were surveyed about their goal-setting habits. Astonishingly, only 3% had documented, specific goals, while the majority had vague aspirations or none at all. Over a decade later, an assessment of their financial status revealed an incredible finding: the 3% with clear objectives had accumulated greater wealth than the remaining 97% combined!

This narrative teaches us two crucial lessons:

1. Clear goals pave the way for significant achievements.
2. Surprisingly, only a small fraction of people actively employ them.

It's likely you're seeking more from life, searching for a means to attain it. You've come to the right place—a resource designed to empower individuals from any background, age, or circumstance to achieve their ambitions.

Within this book, you'll discover three pivotal sections:

1. Crafting precise and meaningful goals
2. Implementing effective strategies to realize those goals
3. Techniques to get motivated and committed

"Can this guide truly help me achieve my aspirations?" Absolutely!

"The Achievement Blueprint" does work—but only when action meets intention. It's the key to unlocking your wishes, provided you're willing to put in the effort.

This book unfolds a detailed, step-by-step pathway demanding your time and dedication to turn aspirations into reality. Merely reading won't suffice! You must actively follow the outlined plan, take decisive action, and leverage the powerful techniques presented.

Trust the process, and I assure you—your dreams will materialize.

CHAPTER 2

The Goal-Getting Process

SELECTING A GOAL

Struggling to pinpoint a goal that resonates with you? Are you overwhelmed by too many options or lack a clear direction? This chapter is tailored just for you!

Yearning for a better life is universal; we all harbor desires. These desires aren't mere wishes—they're wishes with vitality and vigor.

Goals outline the journey to your destination but often lack the spark to ignite your passion and push you forward.

Wishes, however, carry a distinct impact—it's like being struck by lightning instead of a mere flicker of light. They unleash your dreams, elevate you to new heights, and connect you with boundless potential and unwavering enthusiasm, enabling you to achieve what might otherwise seem beyond imagination.

To actualize your aspirations, shift your focus from goals to fulfilling your wishes.

Yet, before making your wishes a reality, the initial step is deciding what exactly to wish for. Many traverse their days day-dreaming about a fulfilling life but struggle to paint a clear picture of what that entails.

Not societal expectations, not others' desires imposed on you, but what genuinely resides in your heart as your aspiration.

DETERMINING THE PRICE

At a gathering, a renowned pianist performed, drawing admiration from the hostess who exclaimed, "I'd do anything to play like you!"

Reflecting for a moment, the pianist responded, "No, you wouldn't."

Surprised, the hostess insisted she would.

The pianist shook her head. "You desire to play as I do now, but are you prepared to devote eight hours a day for twenty years to achieve that proficiency?"

"Take whatever you want, but pay for it," a Spanish proverb advises.

Every wish entails a price. You can attain anything if you're willing to pay. It might demand time, money, or sacrifices you're ready to make.

Your readiness to pay that price determines your capability to turn your wishes into reality. If you're 100% committed to paying, success becomes almost certain.

Commit to paying the price, and watch your wishes unfold into reality.

STRENGTHENING DESIRE

"Desire is the cornerstone, the initial stride towards accomplishing a goal."

Ever set personal or business goals only to falter on the path to achievement? Here's a pivotal question: WHY?

The answer is rather straightforward: our desire wasn't potent enough.

Some may contest this notion. "But I was deeply driven and still fell short." Regrettably, that fervor wasn't forceful enough.

So, how do you recognize intense desire, true passion?

It's what propels individuals to work tirelessly, from early hours until late at night. It dominates conversations, thoughts, and actions.

Pause and consider the goals you've set for yourself. How resolute are you in pursuing them?

Under what circumstances would you consider abandoning them?

Imagine if you could escalate your desire to reach these goals significantly.

What if your longing for them was so intense that quitting was inconceivable? A conviction so absolute that you'd forge a path, no matter what.

When you're genuinely 100% committed to your goals, you shift from merely hoping to knowing.

If you desire something fervently, giving up becomes unthinkable. You either unearth a way forward or create one. You pay the price, whatever it takes.

By nurturing intense desire, the seemingly impossible can become your reality.

CULTIVATING BELIEF

A goal remains a distant dream if you don't believe in your capability to achieve it. Just as neglecting to chart a course or undertake necessary actions renders it unrealized.

Doubt corrodes your commitment. It might even lead you to shelve your ambitions. To wholly achieve anything, you must believe in its possibility at your core.

Belief precedes sight. Seeing is believing.

Should you embrace the idea that success is attainable and enjoyable, and commit to an exhilarating path toward your goals, success becomes an inevitable reality.

DEFINING YOUR PURPOSE

In May 1961, John F. Kennedy pledged America's lunar landing by the decade's end. It stood as a courageous and grand objective, among the greatest in history.

However, merely stating the ambition didn't ensure its realization.

Achieving the moon landing necessitated intelligence, research, planning, resources, people, risk, and unwavering commitment. The crucial step wasn't Neil Armstrong's landing; it was John F. Kennedy defining the Objective.

We define the Objective as the ultimate goal that all your efforts aim toward. For instance, in Investing, it might be reaching $5 million by retirement.

While some may opt for a single Objective, most successful individuals set goals in various spheres:

- Career
- Family
- Financial
- Health
- Knowledge
- Material
- Retirement
- Spiritual

These represent a few categories warranting Objective setting. Objectives are typically long-term, possibly lifelong, though not mandatory. They must hold significance for you and be worth pursuing, or else initiating a goal-setting routine wouldn't be worthwhile.

When starting, initiate by setting Objectives in one or two areas. As small successes accumulate, you'll likely expand to encompass more aspects of your life.

Remember, be bold:

Ensure your Objectives are as ambitious as you can realistically realize. Make certain your goals are S.M.A.R.T.!!! Commit to crafting SMART goals and commence your journey towards them today.

DOCUMENTING YOUR GOALS

Writing down your goal in complete detail holds immense importance.

Words are the vehicle of thought. They impart images, emotions, and sensations to the mind. When encapsulated in words, abstract ideas gain substance and shape.

It ceases to be a fleeting thought—it becomes palpable, stirring motivation or evoking a visceral feeling.

The mechanical act of writing solidifies this process. Transferring these expressions—those thoughts clothed in words—onto paper renders them tangible. The coordination of eye and hand engraves the phrase or expression deeper into our consciousness.

Reading and re-reading this written expression deepens the impression on the mind.

Written goals are directives to the unconscious mind, which adheres to them without question. There's an almost mystical quality to writing down goals, making their achievement nearly certain. The key lies in crafting goals in a way that enhances the likelihood of their fulfillment.

Write it down or bid it farewell.

SETTING A DEADLINE

Establishing a deadline for your goal is akin to igniting the missile of goal-seeking in your mind. Ensure the date is realistic —neither too immediate to be unattainable nor so distant that it lacks urgency. Write this deadline beside your goal and refrain from altering it once set.

Setting a deadline crystallizes thinking and bolsters motivation. However, deadlines alone don't work miracles.

Placing a deadline without a strategy or a realistic plan tied to your present circumstances won't magically deliver results. Deadlines propel us into action.

Failing to assign a deadline relegates the goal to the "as soon as possible" pile, likely never to be pursued. Why? Because amidst our myriad tasks, goals lacking deadlines languish in priority. Goals with deadlines demand attention and action.

DEFINING YOUR REASONS

In the realm of goal setting, many stumble not due to inability but for the lack of clear reasons to forge ahead.

Don't let this impede your progress. Deliberate deeply on why you seek a particular Objective and document your decision.

Why do you desire $5 million at retirement? Why the aspiration for a mansion? The more compelling your reasons, the greater the likelihood of meeting your Objectives.

Conversely, if reasons fail to surface, reconsider your Objective. Absent strong reasons, the goal is unlikely to materialize.

Each person's reasons vary. What one perceives as trivial, another may regard as significant. Your reasons must resonate honestly, and strongly, and serve as genuine motivation.

Record these reasons alongside the relevant Objective, allowing space for expansion or addition. The more reasons, the better —ensuring they authentically represent your desires.

CRAFTING SUB-GOALS

Once you've articulated your Objective and the compelling Reasons behind it, the next pivotal step involves charting the course towards that Objective.

Ask yourself, "What specific steps do I need to take to reach my Objective?" These steps form your Subgoals.

Let's say your Objective is accumulating $5 million by retirement, which might span two decades or more. To achieve this, you'll need a plan. Do you require investment knowledge? Will you need to save a specific amount weekly? Should you consider a career change? These actions that advance your Objective are your Subgoals.

Sub-goals can vary in specificity but must invariably align with your Objective. Equally crucial, each Sub-goal should possess a deadline—a date that not only motivates action but also ensures progression towards your Objective.

It's common to juggle multiple Sub-goals simultaneously. Some Subgoals might not crystallize immediately, appearing as you progress through existing ones.

Writing down Subgoals alongside their Accomplishment Dates is critical. Avoid making Subgoals overly daunting or prolonged to prevent feeling overwhelmed. Break down long-term Subgoals into manageable parts and adjust them upon completion.

By establishing realistic and manageable Sub-goals and consistently meeting their deadlines, you'll steadily make headway toward Objectives that might otherwise seem daunting or unattainable.

DEFINING TASK BREAKDOWNS

Just as Subgoals support Objectives, Tasks further dissect Subgoals into manageable components, making goal setting truly effective. Tasks usually encompass the simple actions imperative to achieve a Subgoal.

For instance, if your Sub-goal is to comprehend bond investments by a certain date, various Tasks contribute to gaining that knowledge.

Tasks might involve actions such as:

- Visiting the library for a book on bonds.
- Devoting time to read the book on specific days.
- Exploring online resources for bond information.
- Seeking advice from an experienced friend in the bond market.

Each Task, documented alongside its associated Subgoal, necessitates an Accomplishment Date. Procrastination or neglecting Tasks can impede Sub-goal achievement within its timeline.

Focus on accomplishing these smaller, manageable Tasks without feeling overwhelmed. Even the briefest Tasks should be noted down and checked off upon completion.

As you consistently complete these Tasks, your confidence and motivation will burgeon. Your belief in your abilities will intensify, fueling your drive to accomplish more.

The secret lies in the first step: the most crucial secret of goal setting. If you're ready to discover it, now's the time to delve in!

CHAPTER 3

Ways to Boost Your Motivation

Success Enhancements encapsulate techniques pivotal to achieving your goals. They revolve around two key elements: effective goal setting and fostering a positive mindset.

SUCCESS QUESTIONS:

Strategic inquiries that guide your focus toward success. Asking questions such as "What can I do today to move closer to my goal?" directs your thoughts and actions, channeling them toward accomplishment.

SUCCESS STIMULANTS:

Activities or habits that boost motivation and productivity. Engaging in exercises, reading inspirational material, or seeking mentorship are stimulants that energize and enhance your journey toward success.

VISUALIZATION TECHNIQUE

Harnessing the power of visual imagery to manifest goals. Your mind processes images, making visualization a potent tool. Seeing yourself in possession of your goals ignites subconscious drives, aligning your actions with the mental images you hold.

The Visualization Technique underscores the brain's propensity to think in images rather than words. It highlights the significance of visualization in manifesting goals and achieving long-term success.

How Visualization Works

1. The Power of Mental Imagery: Your mind processes thoughts through images. Vividly imagining your desired outcome influences your subconscious mind, shaping your actions to align with that mental image.
2. The Impact on Subconscious Behavior: Detailed mental images create a reality for your subconscious mind. Continually visualizing yourself achieving your goal ingrains it into your subconscious, compelling actions that correspond with that mental picture.

3. Making the Unseen Real: Your subconscious cannot differentiate between vividly imagined and real experiences. Consistent visualization reinforces the belief in your ability to attain the goal, translating into actions that materialize that vision.

AFFIRMATION TECHNIQUE

Affirmations involve verbal suggestions directed toward oneself. They wield influence by shaping beliefs and thought patterns, ultimately impacting behavior.

Utilizing self-affirmations to shape beliefs and behaviors. Repeating positive statements reinforces desired traits or outcomes. Craft affirmations aligned with your goals to mold your mindset toward success.

The Role of Affirmations

1. Shaping Self-Beliefs: Repeated affirmations foster beliefs, gradually ingraining them into your subconscious. Positive self-talk influences your self-perception and capabilities.
2. Transforming Negative Self-Talk: By consciously redirecting negative self-talk into positive affirmations, you alter self-perceptions. Changing phrases like "I can't" into affirmations like "I am capable" reshapes your mindset.
3. Aligning with Goal Setting: Tailor affirmations to complement your goals. They serve as reinforcement, aiding in behavioral shifts required to accomplish set objectives.

In summary, by employing Success Enhancements like Visualization and Affirmations in tandem with effective goal-setting practices, you empower your mind to steer actions, beliefs, and behaviors toward realizing your aspirations.